Magnets and Springs

By the end of this book you will know more about:

- Attraction and repulsion between magnets.
- Which materials are attracted to magnets.
- Springs and elastic bands.

You will:

- Use books, CD-ROMs and the Internet for research.
- Carry out fair test investigations.
- Classify materials.

⭐ **Forces are pushes or pulls that make things move, stop, change direction or change shape.**

Task 1 *Forces in action*

✴ What can you remember about forces?

✴ Look at the picture on page 3.

✴ How many examples of forces in action can you see?

Look out for these things:

- Pushing

- Pulling

- Changing direction

- Stopping

- Starting to move

✴ Put a ring around each force in action on Task Sheet 1.

As well as getting things moving and making them stop or change direction, forces can also make things change shape.

There are forces between magnets. Magnets can attract (pull towards) and repel (push away from) each other.

North pole and south pole

A magnet has a south pole at one end and a north pole at the other end. You can find out which end is the north pole by following these instructions.

YOU NEED:

two bar magnets

paper

compass

cotton and Sellotape

Blu-tack

✴ Make a paper sling like the one shown in the picture.

✴ Put a bar magnet into the sling.

✴ Place a compass underneath the magnet, but not too close to it.

✴ Watch the magnet – it will slowly spin until one end is pointing north.
That end is the north pole of the magnet.
Put a small piece of Blu-tack on that end.

✴ The other end of the magnet is the south pole.

✴ Now do the same for a second bar magnet.

⚠ *Do not put your compass too near the magnet.*

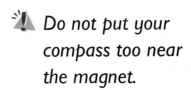

Task 3 *Magnet against magnet*

....

 Now that you have found the north pole on each of your magnets, find out what happens if you put:

- north pole against north pole
- south pole against south pole
- north pole against south pole
- south pole against north pole

 Write down a set of rules that explains what you have to do to make:

- magnets attract (pull) each other
- magnets repel (push) each other

For example:

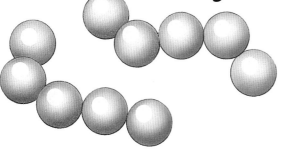

If you put the north pole of one magnet against the north pole of another magnet, they will ———— each other.

Magnetic marbles

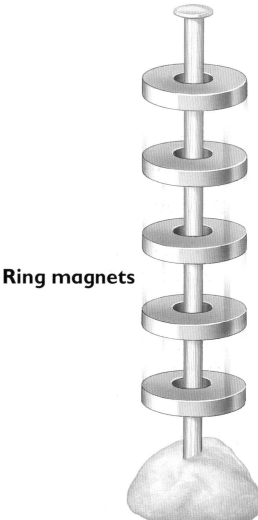

Ring magnets

 How do you think magnetic marbles work?
What do you think they look like inside?

 Why do these ring magnets bounce off each other?
What could you do to make them stick together?

Some materials are magnetic, but others are not. Make and test predictions.

 # Magnets

- Magnets attract certain materials.
- Materials that are attracted to magnets are called magnetic.
- Iron and steel are magnetic metals. Objects containing these metals are attracted to a magnet.
- Other metals are not magnetic. Gold, silver, copper and aluminium are not attracted to a magnet.

 Task **4** *Is it magnetic?*

2

🔸 Which of the objects do you think will be attracted to the magnet?

🔸 What will you do to test your prediction?

🔸 How will you record your results?

🔸 Were your predictions correct?

YOU NEED:

bar magnet

screw

pencil rubber

5 pence piece

2 pence piece

scissors

nail

drink can

paper-clip

pencil

button

wooden ruler

- Collect 15 different objects from around the classroom.

- Find out whether your objects are magnetic.

- What material is each object made from?

- Record your results in the table on Task Sheet 2

Object	Material made from	Is it magnetic?	Explanation
book	paper	no	does not contain iron or steel

YOU NEED:

bar magnet

15 classroom objects

Do not test electrical things or watches to see if they are magnetic.

- What have you learned about magnetic materials?
  What have you learned about non-magnetic materials?

- Make up a poem about magnets to help you remember why some materials are magnetic and others are not.

Magnets have many different uses.

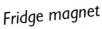 Task
5 *Useful magnets*
....

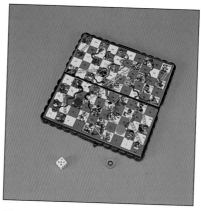
Travel game

Fridge magnet

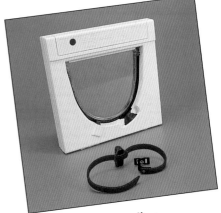
Cat flap and collar

 Where have you seen magnets used?
What were they used for?
Make a list like this:

Where seen	What magnets were used for
travel game	to hold pieces onto board

Sketch a design for a fridge magnet.

Write a set of instructions for making your fridge magnet.
Draw pictures to illustrate your instructions
What materials would you use?

Make and test your fridge magnet.
How many sheets of paper can it hold on to the fridge?

YOU NEED:

cardboard and other materials

magnets

transparent jar, plastic lemonade bottle or fish bowl filled with water.

paper-clips and drawing pins

string

drinking straw

Task 6 *Magnetic toys*

Make one of these toys and write a set of instructions to show someone else how to make the toy. Explain how the toy works.

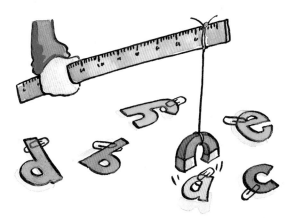

- **Magnetic fishing game** to help younger children to learn letters and numbers.

- **Magnetic diver and fish**. How will you make the diver go up and down in the water?

How to make a magnetic fishing game

- **Magnetic animal**. How will you make your animal move?

Make your talk interesting

In the canteen at Star Ltd, the staff are losing a lot of knives, forks and spoons.

They are being thrown away, by accident, with the scraps of food.

✺ On Task Sheet 3 design something to stop this happening.

✺ Make and test your design using paper-clips instead of knives, forks and spoons.

✺ The directors at Star Ltd would like to know what can be done about this problem.
In your group, give a talk to the class explaining how you solved the problem. How will you show them in an interesting way?

Task 8 *Researching magnets*

 What else can you find out about magnets?

 Get into groups and brainstorm questions about magnets.

Questions about magnets:

How are magnets made?

Where are magnets used?

Who discovered magnets?

 Where could you look for information to find out the answers to your questions?

 When you have found your answers, find an interesting way of telling other people about magnets and their amazing powers. For example, you could make one of the following:

Poster

Book

Advert

Plan and carry out a fair test to investigate magnets.

Scientific Enquiry

Magnet questions

4

Draw a diagram like this one on Task Sheet 4. On your diagram, write 5 questions about magnets that you could investigate using a fair test.

Which magnet is the strongest?

MAGNETS

Our results tell us that...

Plan and carry out a fair test to answer one of the questions on your diagram.

How can you make sure that you use measurement in your investigation?

How will you record your results?

In a speech bubble, write the answer to your question.

Magnets concept map

5

★ Look back through your work to remind yourself what you have learned about magnets so far.

★ Make a concept map on Task Sheet 5 using these words:

like	attract	pull	unlike	magnets
repel	stronger	materials	north poles	metals
weaker	force	push	south poles	iron and steel

Remember, you must write along the arrows to show the links between the words in the boxes.

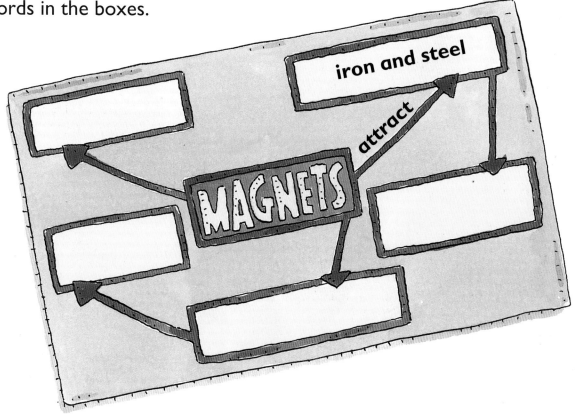

Springs are used in everyday objects.

What does the spring do?

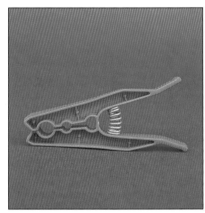

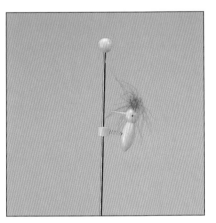

Did you know that there are springs in all sorts of objects?

These pictures show objects that use springs.

 Write down what you think the springs do.

Make a list of other objects that use springs.

⭐ **Springs can be stretched (pulled out longer) or compressed (squashed smaller).**

 Task 11 *Feel the force*

YOU NEED:

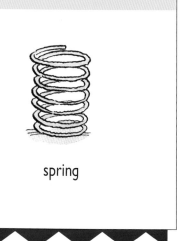

spring

⚠ *Be careful when pulling and squashing springs.*

✴ Hold the spring with both hands. Gently stretch the spring by pulling it.

✴ In a speech bubble, explain what forces (pushes or pulls) you can feel when you stretch the spring.

Words to learn and use:
compress
force
pull
push
spring
stretch

When I stretch the spring...

✴ Place the spring on the palm of your hand. Gently compress the spring by pushing down on it with your other hand.

✴ In a speech bubble, explain what forces (pushes or pulls) you can feel when you compress the spring.

When I compress the spring...

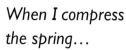

Forces are in action when we stretch or compress a spring.

 Task **12** *Forces in action*

....

 6

⚠ *Be careful when using staplers.*

These photographs show where the springs are in a retractable pen, a hole punch and a stapler.

YOU NEED:

stapler

hole punch

transparent retractable pen

✪ Try each object out to see how they work.

✪ Complete the sentences on Task Sheet 6 to explain what the springs do to make make each object work.

In the stapler, the spring . . .

In the hole punch, the springs . . .

In the retractable pen, the spring . . .

Plan and carry out a fair test to investigate the stretchiness of springs.

Scientific Enquiry

How stretchy?

 7

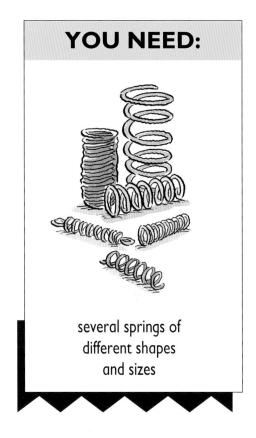

YOU NEED:

several springs of different shapes and sizes

✦ Plan and carry out a fair test to investigate the stretchiness of different springs.

✦ Use Task Sheet 7 to help you.

✦ How will you measure stretchiness?

✦ How will you make sure that your test is fair?

✦ Put the springs in order to show how stretchy you think they will be, with the most stretchy first and the least stretchy last. Write your predictions down. Explain your predictions.

✦ Now carry out your test. Were your predictions correct?

Feel the forces when you stretch an elastic band.

Just imagine ...

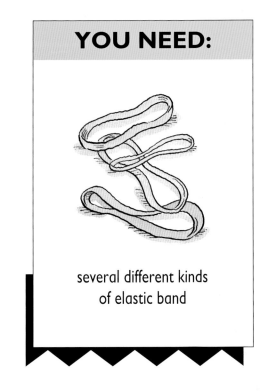

YOU NEED:

several different kinds
of elastic band

 Gently stretch each of the elastic bands.
What do you feel?

 Never flick an elastic band at anyone.

 Imagine that you are a tiny part of an
elastic band.
What happens when you are stretched and
when you are let go?

> It's funny being a piece
> of elastic band. When
> someone picks me up and
> begins to pull ...

 Copy this thought bubble.
Complete the sentence to explain what
happens to you.

⭐ Investigate what happens when you stretch elastic bands by different amounts.

Scientific Enquiry
Stretch investigation

- Plan and carry out a fair test to investigate how the stretch of the elastic band affects the distance the car travels.

- Use Task Sheet 8 to help you.

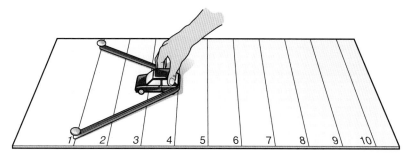

YOU NEED:

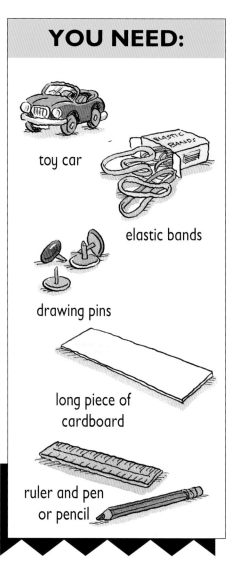

toy car

elastic bands

drawing pins

long piece of cardboard

ruler and pen or pencil

- Record the results of your test on a table like this:

Amount of stretch	Distance car travelled

The numbers on the table . . .

Our conclusion is . . .

The pattern of the results shows . . .

If we double the stretch to 20, the . . .

- Look at your table of results.
  Copy the speech bubbles below.
  Use the information in your table to complete the sentences.

Bungee jumping
....

Stretchiness can be used for unusual things, such as bungee jumping.

Bungee jumpers leap off high places with a piece of stretchy cord attached to their legs.

A bungee jump

✦ What do you think happens when this person jumps?
Use what you have learned so far about springs and elastic bands to explain how bungee jumping works.

⭐ **Plan and carry out a fair test to investigate how the size of the force affects the stretch.**

(Task 17) **Scientific Enquiry**
Bungee investigation

a

◇ How do you think the mass of a bungee jumper affects how far the person bounces? Make a prediction.

◇ Plan and carry out a fair test to investigate your prediction using an elastic band and everyday objects.

◇ Use Task Sheet 9 to help you.

◇ How will you record your results?

◇ Look at your results. Was your prediction correct?

Checkpoint 2

Springs concept map

⬙ Look back through your work to remind yourself what you have learned about springs and elastic bands.

⬙ Make a concept map on Task Sheet 10 using these words:

springs   **stretchiness**   **pushes**   **forces**   **pulls**

compress   **stretch**   **material**   **elastic bands**   **direction**

size of force

Remember, you must write along the arrows to show the links between the words in the boxes.

Summary

Which of these do you know and which can you do?

- I know that there are forces between magnets, and that magnets can attract or repel each other.
- I know that some materials are magnetic, but others are not.
- I know that magnets have many different uses.
- I can plan and carry out a fair test to investigate magnets and the stretchiness of springs.
- I know that springs are used in everyday objects.
- I know that springs can be stretched or compressed.
- I know that forces are in action when we stretch or compress a spring.
- I can feel the forces when I stretch an elastic band and compress or stretch a spring.
- I can make and test predictions.

Complete your **Science Log** to show how well you know these and how well you can do them. Circle a face for each statement.

Glossary

force

attract - to pull something so that it comes nearer.

compress - to squash smaller.

compress

elastic band - a loop of material that can stretch and then go back to its usual size.

force - a push or a pull.

magnet - a metal object that can make pieces of iron or steel stick to it.

magnetic - able to be attracted by a magnet.

non-magnetic - unable to be attracted by a magnet.

pole - either of the two ends of a magnet.

repel - to push something away.

spring - a piece of metal wound into a spiral or bent so that it bounces back into shape after it is compressed or stretched.

stretch - to pull something so that it becomes longer.

stretch